THE COOKIE

Delicious cookies, treats

Publications International, Ltd.

Pictured on the front cover (*clockwise from top left*): Tiny Peanut Butter Sandwiches *(page 10),* Double Mint Cookies *(page 34),* Linzer Sandwich Cookies *(page 54),* and Buttery Almond Cutouts *(page 104).*

Pictured on the back cover (*clockwise from left)*: Jolly Peanut Butter Gingerbread Cookies *(page 110),* Decadent Coconut Macaroons *(page 50),* and One-Bite Chocolate Chip Cookies *(page 4).*

ISBN: 978-1-68022-083-4

Library of Congress Control Number: 2015938504

Manufactured in China.

8 7 6 5 4 3 2 1

Microwave Cooking: Microwave ovens vary in wattage. Use the cooking times as guidelines and check for doneness before adding more time.

Preparation/Cooking Times: Preparation times are based on the approximate amount of time required to assemble the recipe before cooking, baking, chilling or serving. These times include preparation steps such as measuring, chopping and mixing. The fact that some preparations and cooking can be done simultaneously is taken into account. Preparation of optional ingredients and serving suggestions is not included.

Publications International, Ltd.

Table of Contents

Cookie Jar Classics

One-Bite Chocolate Chip Cookies

Makes about 14 dozen cookies

1¼ cups all-purpose flour
½ teaspoon baking soda
¼ teaspoon salt
½ cup packed light brown sugar
½ cup (1 stick) butter, softened

¼ cup granulated sugar
1 egg
1 teaspoon vanilla
1¼ cups mini semisweet chocolate chips
Sea salt (optional)

1. Preheat oven to 350°F.

2. Whisk flour, baking soda and salt in medium bowl. Beat brown sugar, butter and granulated sugar in large bowl with electric mixer at medium speed until light and fluffy. Beat in egg and vanilla until blended. Add flour mixture; beat at low speed until well blended. Stir in chocolate chips.

3. Drop dough by ½ teaspoonfuls 1 inch apart onto ungreased cookie sheets. Sprinkle very lightly with sea salt, if desired.

4. Bake 6 minutes or just until edges are lightly browned. (Centers of cookies will be very light and will not look done.) Cool on cookie sheets 2 minutes. Remove to wire racks; cool completely.

Butter Pecan Crisps

Makes about 5 dozen cookies

1 cup (2 sticks) unsalted
butter, softened
¾ cup granulated sugar
¾ cup packed brown sugar
½ teaspoon salt
2 eggs
1½ cups finely ground pecans

1 teaspoon vanilla
2½ cups sifted all-purpose flour
1 teaspoon baking soda
30 pecan halves
4 squares (1 ounce each)
semisweet chocolate
1 tablespoon shortening

1. Preheat oven to 375°F. Line cookie sheets with parchment paper.

2. Beat butter, granulated sugar, brown sugar and salt in large bowl with electric mixer at medium speed until light and fluffy. Add eggs, one at a time, beating well after each addition. Beat in ground pecans and vanilla. Combine flour and baking soda in small bowl. Gradually add flour mixture to butter mixture, beating well after each addition.

3. Spoon dough into large pastry bag fitted with ⅜-inch round tip; fill bag halfway. Shake down dough to remove air bubbles. Hold bag about ½ inch above prepared cookie sheets. Pipe dough into 1¼-inch balls, spacing 3 inches apart. Cut each pecan half lengthwise into 2 slivers. Press 1 sliver in center of each ball.

4. Bake 10 minutes or until lightly browned. Cool on cookie sheets 5 minutes. Remove to wire racks; cool completely.

5. Melt chocolate and shortening in small heavy saucepan over low heat; stir until blended. Drizzle chocolate mixture over cookies. Let stand until set.

Lemon Poppy Seed Cookies

Makes 2 dozen cookies

1 cup sugar
½ cup (1 stick) unsalted butter,
   softened
1 egg
2 tablespoons grated lemon
   peel

2 tablespoons poppy seeds
¼ teaspoon vanilla
1¾ cups all-purpose flour
¼ teaspoon salt

1. Beat sugar and butter in medium bowl with electric mixer at medium speed until light and fluffy. Beat in egg, lemon peel, poppy seeds and vanilla until well blended. Add flour and salt; beat just until blended. Shape dough into disc; wrap and refrigerate 1 hour.

2. Preheat oven to 325°F. Lightly grease or line cookie sheets with parchment paper.

3. Shape dough by tablespoonfuls into 1-inch balls. Place 2 inches apart on prepared cookie sheets.

4. Bake 15 minutes or until set. Cool on cookie sheets 2 minutes. Remove to wire racks; cool completely.

Tip

Cookies that are uniform in size and shape will finish baking at the same time. To easily shape drop cookies into a uniform size, use an ice cream scoop with a release bar.

Tiny Peanut Butter Sandwiches

Makes 6 to 7 dozen sandwiches

1¼ cups all-purpose flour
½ teaspoon baking powder
½ teaspoon baking soda
¼ teaspoon salt
½ cup granulated sugar
½ cup packed brown sugar
½ cup (1 stick) butter, softened

½ cup creamy peanut butter
1 egg
1 teaspoon vanilla
1 cup semisweet chocolate
   chips
½ cup whipping cream

1. Preheat oven to 350°F.

2. Whisk flour, baking powder, baking soda and salt in medium bowl. Beat granulated sugar, brown sugar and butter in large bowl with electric mixer at medium speed until light and fluffy. Beat in peanut butter, egg and vanilla until well blended. Gradually add flour mixture, beating at low speed until blended.

3. Shape dough by ½ teaspoonfuls into balls; place 1 inch apart on ungreased cookie sheets. Flatten balls slightly in crisscross pattern with tines of fork.

4. Bake 6 minutes or until set. Cool on cookie sheets 4 minutes. Remove to wire racks; cool completely.

5. Meanwhile, place chocolate chips in medium heatproof bowl. Place cream in small microwavable bowl. Microwave on HIGH 2 minutes or just until simmering; pour over chocolate chips. Let stand 2 minutes; stir until smooth. Let stand 10 minutes or until filling thickens to desired consistency.

6. Spread scant teaspoonful of filling on flat sides of half of cookies; top with remaining cookies.

Mexican Sugar Cookies

Makes about 5 dozen cookies

2½ cups shortening
2 cups sugar, divided
1 teaspoon ground anise
2 eggs
¼ cup orange juice
6 cups all-purpose flour

1 tablespoon baking powder
½ teaspoon cream of tartar
½ teaspoon salt
3 tablespoons ground cinnamon

1. Beat shortening, 1 cup sugar and anise in large bowl with electric mixer at medium speed until light and fluffy. Add eggs, one at a time, beating well after each addition. Add orange juice; beat until light and fluffy.

2. Whisk flour, baking powder, cream of tartar and salt in medium bowl. Gradually add to shortening mixture, beating well after each addition.

3. Knead dough on lightly floured surface. Shape dough into two discs; wrap and refrigerate 30 minutes.

4. Preheat oven to 350°F. Lightly grease or line cookie sheets with parchment paper.

5. Working with one disc at a time, roll out dough between sheets of parchment paper to ½-inch thickness. Cut out shapes with cookie cutters. Gently press dough trimmings together; reroll and cut out additional cookies. Place 2 inches apart on prepared cookie sheets.

6. Bake 5 to 8 minutes or until lightly browned. Remove from oven. Combine remaining 1 cup sugar and cinnamon in small bowl. Sprinkle warm cookies with cinnamon-sugar mixture. Cool completely on wire racks.

Triple Ginger Cookies

Makes 3 dozen cookies

2 cups all-purpose flour
2 teaspoons baking soda
1 teaspoon ground ginger
½ teaspoon salt
¾ cup (1½ sticks) unsalted butter
1¼ cups sugar, divided
¼ cup light molasses
1 egg
1 tablespoon finely minced fresh ginger

1 tablespoon finely minced crystallized ginger*

Semisoft sugar-coated ginger slices are preferable to the small dry ginger cubes found in the supermarket spice shelves. The softer, larger slices are available at natural foods or specialty stores. If using the small dry cubes of ginger, steep the cubes in boiling hot water a few minutes to soften. Drain the cubes, then pat dry and mince.

1. Sift flour, baking soda, ground ginger and salt onto waxed paper. Melt butter in small heavy saucepan over low heat; pour into large bowl and cool slightly. Add 1 cup sugar, molasses and egg; mix well. Add flour mixture; mix well. Add fresh ginger and crystallized ginger; stir just until blended. Cover; refrigerate 1 hour.

2. Preheat oven to 375°F. Lightly grease or line cookie sheets with parchment paper.

3. Shape dough by tablespoonfuls into 1-inch balls. Roll in remaining ¼ cup sugar. Place 3 inches apart on prepared cookie sheets. (If dough is very sticky, drop by teaspoonfuls into sugar to coat.)

4. For chewy cookies, bake 7 minutes or until edges are lightly browned. For crispier cookies, bake 9 to 11 minutes. Cool on cookie sheets 1 minute. Remove to wire racks; cool completely.

Variation: Roll dough in plastic wrap to form a log. Refrigerate up to 1 week or freeze up to 2 months. To bake, bring the dough almost to room temperature. Slice dough into ¼-inch-thick slices; dip the tops in sugar. Bake as directed above.

Orange-Almond Sables

Makes about 2 dozen cookies

1½ cups powdered sugar
1 cup (2 sticks) butter, softened
1 tablespoon finely grated orange peel
1 tablespoon almond-flavored liqueur *or* 1 teaspoon almond extract
¾ cup whole blanched almonds, toasted*

1¾ cups all-purpose flour
¼ teaspoon salt
1 egg, beaten

To toast almonds, spread in single layer on baking sheet. Bake in preheated 375°F oven 5 to 7 minutes or until golden brown, stirring frequently.

1. Preheat oven to 375°F. Beat powdered sugar and butter in large bowl with electric mixer at medium speed until light and fluffy. Beat in orange peel and liqueur.

2. Reserve 24 whole almonds. Place remaining cooled almonds in food processor or blender; process using on/off pulsing action until almonds are ground but not pasty.

3. Whisk ground almonds, flour and salt in medium bowl. Gradually add to butter mixture, beating with electric mixer at low speed until well blended after each addition.

4. Roll out dough between sheets of parchment paper to ¼-inch thickness. Cut out shapes with 2½-inch fluted or round cookie cutter. Place 2 inches apart on ungreased cookie sheets. Press 1 whole reserved almond in center of each shape. Lightly brush with egg.

5. Bake 10 minutes or until lightly browned. Cool on cookie sheets 1 minute. Remove to wire racks; cool completely.

Browned Butter Spritz Cookies

Makes about 8 dozen cookies

1½ cups (3 sticks) unsalted butter
½ cup granulated sugar
¼ cup powdered sugar
1 egg yolk

1 teaspoon vanilla
⅛ teaspoon almond extract
2½ cups all-purpose flour
¼ cup cake flour
¼ teaspoon salt

1. Melt butter in medium heavy saucepan over medium heat until light amber, stirring frequently. Transfer butter to large bowl. Cover and refrigerate 2 hours or until solid.

2. Let browned butter stand at room temperature 15 minutes. Preheat oven to 350°F.

3. Beat browned butter, granulated sugar and powdered sugar in large bowl with electric mixer at medium speed until light and fluffy. Add egg yolk, vanilla and almond extract; beat until well blended. Whisk all-purpose flour, cake flour and salt in small bowl. Add flour mixture to butter mixture; beat until well blended.

4. Fit cookie press with desired plate (or change plates for different shapes after first batch). Fill press with dough; press dough 1 inch apart on ungreased cookie sheets.

5. Bake 10 minutes or until lightly browned. Cool on cookie sheets 5 minutes. Remove to wire racks; cool completely.

Tip

To add holiday sparkle to these delicious cookies, press red or green glacé cherry halves into the centers or sprinkle them with colored sugar or nonpareils before baking. To add more color to the cookies, tint the dough with green food coloring before pressing and pipe red icing bows on the baked and cooled cookies.

Butter-Nut Chocolate Topped Cookies

Makes about 2½ dozen cookies

½ cup (1 stick) butter or margarine, softened
½ cup sugar
1 egg
1 teaspoon vanilla extract
1¼ cups all-purpose flour

¼ teaspoon baking soda
⅛ teaspoon salt
30 HERSHEY'S® KISSES®BRAND Milk Chocolates
½ cup ground almonds, pecans or walnuts

1. Beat butter, sugar, egg and vanilla in medium bowl until well blended. Stir together flour, baking soda and salt; add to butter mixture, beating well. If necessary, refrigerate dough until firm enough to handle.

2. Remove wrappers from chocolates. Heat oven to 350°F. Shape dough into 1-inch balls; roll in ground nuts. Place on ungreased cookie sheet.

3. Bake 10 to 12 minutes or until almost no imprint remains when touched lightly in center. Remove from oven; immediately press a chocolate into center of each cookie. Carefully remove from cookie sheet to wire rack. Cool completely. Chocolate should be set before storing.

Orange Variation: Add ¾ teaspoon freshly grated orange peel to butter mixture.

Chunkies & Chewies

Chocolate Chunk Cookies

Makes 2 dozen cookies

1⅔ cups all-purpose flour
⅓ cup CREAM OF WHEAT® Hot Cereal (Instant, 1-minute, 2½-minute or 10-minute cook time), uncooked
½ teaspoon baking soda
¼ teaspoon salt
¾ cup (1½ sticks) butter, softened

½ cup packed brown sugar
⅓ cup granulated sugar
1 egg
1 teaspoon vanilla extract
1 (11.5-ounce) bag chocolate chunks
1 cup chopped pecans

1. Preheat oven to 375°F. Lightly grease cookie sheets. Blend flour, Cream of Wheat, baking soda and salt in medium bowl; set aside.

2. Beat butter and sugars in large bowl with electric mixer at medium speed until creamy. Add egg and vanilla. Beat until fluffy. Reduce speed to low. Add Cream of Wheat mixture; mix well. Stir in chocolate chunks and pecans.

3. Drop by tablespoonfuls onto prepared cookie sheets. Bake 9 to 11 minutes or until golden brown. Let stand on cookie sheets 1 minute before transferring to wire racks to cool completely.

Prep Time: 15 minutes • Start-to-Finish Time: 35 minutes

Ginger Raisin Cookies

Makes about 2 dozen cookies

1½ cups all-purpose flour
1 teaspoon baking soda
1 teaspoon ground ginger
1 teaspoon grated orange
  peel
½ teaspoon salt
½ teaspoon ground cinnamon
¾ cup granulated sugar,
  divided

½ cup packed brown sugar
½ cup (1 stick) butter, softened
1 egg
3 tablespoons molasses
1 teaspoon vanilla
1 cup raisins

1. Preheat oven to 375°F. Lightly grease or line cookie sheets with parchment paper.

2. Whisk flour, baking soda, ginger, orange peel, salt and cinnamon in medium bowl. Beat ½ cup granulated sugar, brown sugar and butter in large bowl with electric mixer at medium speed 2 minutes or until light and fluffy. Add egg, molasses and vanilla; beat 1 minute. Add flour mixture and raisins; stir until blended.

3. Shape dough by tablespoonfuls into 1-inch balls. Roll in remaining ¼ cup granulated sugar. Place 1½ inches apart on prepared cookie sheets.

4. Bake 10 minutes or until edges are set and centers are still slightly soft. Cool on cookie sheets 2 minutes. Remove to wire racks; cool completely.

Cranberry Cookies

Makes about 6 dozen cookies

1 cup (2 sticks) butter
¾ cup packed brown sugar
1 package (4-serving size)
   vanilla instant pudding mix
¼ cup granulated sugar
1 teaspoon ground cinnamon
1 teaspoon vanilla

½ teaspoon ground nutmeg
2 eggs
2¼ cups all-purpose flour
1 teaspoon baking soda
1 package (9 ounces) dried
   cranberries

1. Preheat oven to 350°F.

2. Beat butter, brown sugar, pudding mix, granulated sugar, cinnamon, vanilla and nutmeg in large bowl with electric mixer at medium speed until light and fluffy. Add eggs, one at a time, beating well after each addition. Gradually add flour and baking soda, beating at low speed until blended.

3. Stir in cranberries. Drop dough by rounded teaspoonfuls onto ungreased cookie sheets.

4. Bake 10 minutes or until lightly browned. Cool on cookie sheets 2 minutes. Remove to wire racks; cool completely.

Chunky Chocolate Chip Peanut Butter Cookies

Makes about 3 dozen cookies

1¼ cups all-purpose flour
½ teaspoon baking soda
½ teaspoon salt
½ teaspoon ground cinnamon
¾ cup (1½ sticks) butter or margarine, softened
½ cup granulated sugar
½ cup packed brown sugar
½ cup creamy peanut butter

1 large egg
1 teaspoon vanilla extract
2 cups (12-ounce package) NESTLÉ® TOLL HOUSE® Semi-Sweet Chocolate Morsels
½ cup coarsely chopped peanuts

PREHEAT oven to 375°F.

COMBINE flour, baking soda, salt and cinnamon in small bowl. Beat butter, granulated sugar, brown sugar and peanut butter in large mixer bowl until creamy. Beat in egg and vanilla extract. Gradually beat in flour mixture. Stir in morsels and peanuts.

DROP dough by rounded tablespoonful onto ungreased baking sheets. Press down slightly to flatten into 2-inch circles.

BAKE for 7 to 10 minutes or until edges are set but centers are still soft. Cool on baking sheets for 4 minutes; remove to wire racks to cool completely.

New England Raisin Spice Cookies

Makes about 5 dozen cookies

1 cup packed brown sugar	1 teaspoon salt
½ cup shortening	¾ teaspoon ground cinnamon
¼ cup (½ stick) butter	¼ teaspoon ground ginger
⅓ cup molasses	¼ teaspoon ground cloves
1 egg	⅛ teaspoon ground allspice
2¼ cups all-purpose flour	1½ cups raisins
2 teaspoons baking soda	Granulated sugar

1. Beat brown sugar, shortening and butter in large bowl with electric mixer at medium speed until light and fluffy. Add molasses and egg; beat until blended.

2. Combine flour, baking soda, salt, cinnamon, ginger, cloves and allspice in medium bowl. Stir in raisins. Gradually add shortening mixture, stirring just until blended. Cover; refrigerate at least 2 hours.

3. Preheat oven to 350°F.

4. Shape dough by heaping tablespoonfuls into balls. Roll in granulated sugar. Place 2 inches apart on ungreased cookie sheets.

5. Bake 8 minutes or until lightly browned. Cool on cookie sheets 1 minute. Remove to wire racks; cool completely.

Chunky Monkey Cookies

Makes 2½ dozen cookies

2⅔ cups all-purpose flour

½ teaspoon baking soda

¼ teaspoon salt

1 cup packed light brown sugar

1 cup (2 sticks) unsalted butter, softened

½ cup granulated sugar

¾ to 1 cup mashed ripe banana* (1 large banana)

1 egg

½ teaspoon banana extract (optional)

1½ cups (8 ounces) coarsely chopped bittersweet chocolate

1 cup coarsely chopped walnuts

Do not use overripe bananas, such as those used in quick breads. The banana flesh should be creamy white, with no brown spots.

1. Preheat oven to 300°F.

2. Whisk flour, baking soda and salt in medium bowl. Beat brown sugar, butter and granulated sugar in large bowl with electric mixer at medium speed until light and fluffy. Add banana, egg and banana extract, if desired; beat just until blended. (Banana chunks should be visible.) Beat in flour mixture just until blended.

3. Fold in chocolate and walnuts. Drop dough by rounded teaspoonfuls 2 inches apart onto ungreased cookie sheets.

4. Bake 20 minutes or until edges are lightly browned. Cool on cookie sheets 2 minutes. Remove to wire racks; cool completely.

Double Mint Cookies

Makes 2½ dozen cookies

2 cups all-purpose flour
½ teaspoon baking powder
½ teaspoon baking soda
½ teaspoon salt
¾ cup granulated sugar
¾ cup packed brown sugar
¼ cup (½ stick) butter,
    softened

2 eggs, beaten
1 teaspoon vanilla
½ cup green mint chips
½ cup coarsely chopped
    peppermint candies

1. Preheat oven to 350°F. Line cookie sheets with parchment paper. Combine flour, baking powder, baking soda and salt in medium bowl; mix well.

2. Beat granulated sugar, brown sugar and butter in large bowl with electric mixer at medium speed until well blended. Add eggs and vanilla; mix well. Add flour mixture; mix well. Stir in mint chips and chopped candy. Shape dough into 1-inch balls; place 3 inches apart on prepared cookie sheets.

3. Bake 10 to 12 minutes or until cookies are golden. Cool 1 minute on cookie sheets. Remove to wire racks; cool completely.

Molasses Spice Cookies

Makes about 2½ dozen cookies

1¾ cups all-purpose flour
1 teaspoon baking soda
1 teaspoon ground ginger
1 teaspoon ground cinnamon
¼ teaspoon ground cloves
¼ teaspoon salt
1 cup granulated sugar
¾ cup (1½ sticks) butter or margarine, softened

1 large egg
¼ cup unsulphured molasses
2 cups (12-ounce package) NESTLÉ® TOLL HOUSE® Premier White Morsels
1 cup finely chopped walnuts

COMBINE flour, baking soda, ginger, cinnamon, cloves and salt in small bowl. Beat sugar and butter in large mixer bowl until creamy. Beat in egg and molasses. Gradually beat in flour mixture. Stir in morsels. Refrigerate for 20 minutes or until slightly firm.

PREHEAT oven to 375°F.

ROLL dough into 1-inch balls; roll in walnuts. Place on ungreased baking sheets.

BAKE for 9 to 11 minutes or until golden brown. Cool on baking sheets for 2 minutes; remove to wire racks to cool completely.

Prep Time: 40 minutes • **Bake Time:** 9 to 11 minutes

Berried Snowballs

Makes 2 dozen snowballs

¼ cup (½ stick) unsalted butter
4 cups mini marshmallows
4 cups crispy rice cereal
¾ to 1 cup sweetened dried
    cranberries

Vegetable oil
1½ cups flaked coconut

1. Melt butter in large heavy saucepan over low heat. Add marshmallows; cook and stir until melted. Remove from heat. (Or place butter and marshmallows in large microwavable bowl. Microwave on HIGH at 30-second intervals, stirring between each interval until melted and smooth.)

2. While mixture is still hot, add cereal and cranberries, stirring until well coated. With lightly oiled fingers, shape mixture into 24 (2-inch) balls. Roll balls in coconut. Let stand until cool.

Tip

Berried Snowballs can be frozen in resealable food storage bags or in airtight containers with waxed paper between the layers.

Island Cookies

Makes about 3 dozen cookies

1⅔ cups all-purpose flour
¾ teaspoon baking powder
½ teaspoon baking soda
½ teaspoon salt
¾ cup (1½ sticks) butter, softened
¾ cup packed brown sugar
⅓ cup granulated sugar

1 teaspoon vanilla extract
1 large egg
1¾ cups (11.5-ounce package) NESTLÉ® TOLL HOUSE® Milk Chocolate Morsels
1 cup flaked coconut, toasted, if desired
1 cup chopped walnuts

PREHEAT oven to 375°F.

COMBINE flour, baking powder, baking soda and salt in small bowl. Beat butter, brown sugar, granulated sugar and vanilla extract in large mixer bowl until creamy. Beat in egg. Gradually beat in flour mixture. Stir in morsels, coconut and nuts. Drop by slightly rounded tablespoonful onto ungreased baking sheets.

BAKE for 8 to 11 minutes or until edges are lightly browned. Cool on baking sheets for 2 minutes; remove to wire racks to cool completely.

Note: NESTLÉ® TOLL HOUSE® Semi-Sweet Chocolate Morsels, Semi-Sweet Chocolate Mini Morsels, Premier White Morsels or Butterscotch Flavored Morsels can be substituted for the Milk Chocolate Morsels.

Top-Notch Treats

Macadamia Nut White Chip Pumpkin Cookies

Makes about 4 dozen cookies

2 cups all-purpose flour
2 teaspoons ground cinnamon
1 teaspoon ground cloves
1 teaspoon baking soda
1 cup (2 sticks) butter or margarine, softened
½ cup granulated sugar
½ cup packed brown sugar

1 cup LIBBY'S® 100% Pure Pumpkin
1 large egg
2 teaspoons vanilla extract
2 cups (12-ounce package) NESTLÉ® TOLL HOUSE® Premier White Morsels
⅔ cup coarsely chopped macadamia nuts or walnuts, toasted

PREHEAT oven to 350°F.

COMBINE flour, cinnamon, cloves and baking soda in small bowl. Beat butter, granulated sugar and brown sugar in large mixer bowl until creamy. Beat in pumpkin, egg and vanilla extract until blended. Gradually beat in flour mixture. Stir in morsels and nuts. Drop by rounded tablespoonful onto greased baking sheets; flatten slightly with back of spoon or greased bottom of glass dipped in granulated sugar.

BAKE for 11 to 14 minutes or until centers are set. Cool on baking sheets for 2 minutes; remove to wire racks to cool completely.

Prep Time: 20 minutes • **Bake Time:** 11 to 14 minutes

Brandy Snaps with Lemon Ricotta Cream

Makes 2 dozen cookies

¾ cup sugar, divided
1 cup (2 sticks) butter, softened, divided
⅓ cup light corn syrup
1 cup all-purpose flour
1 tablespoon brandy or cognac

½ cup ricotta cheese
1 tablespoon lemon juice
2 teaspoons grated lemon peel

1. Preheat oven to 325°F.

2. Combine ½ cup sugar, ½ cup butter and corn syrup in medium saucepan; cook and stir over medium heat until butter is melted. Stir in flour and brandy. Drop batter by level tablespoonfuls about 3 inches apart onto ungreased cookie sheets, spacing to fit 4 cookies per sheet.

3. Bake, one cookie sheet at a time, 12 minutes or until lightly browned. Cool on cookie sheets 1 minute. Remove each cookie and quickly wrap around handle of wooden spoon.

4. Combine remaining ½ cup butter, ¼ cup sugar, ricotta, lemon juice and lemon peel in food processor or blender; process until smooth. Place filling in pastry bag fitted with plain or star tip. Fill cookies just before serving.

Tip

Unsalted butter has a more delicate flavor and is preferred by many cooks, especially for baking. Although it varies by manufacturer, salted butter has about 1½ teaspoons added salt per pound. Do not substitute whipped butter for regular butter in baked goods.

Chocolate Peppermint Macaroons

Makes 2 dozen macaroons

½ cup (4 ounces) chopped bittersweet chocolate

2 squares (1 ounce each) unsweetened chocolate

2 egg whites

⅛ teaspoon salt

½ cup sugar

½ teaspoon peppermint extract

2¾ cups flaked coconut

½ cup finely crushed peppermint candies*

*About 18 peppermint candies will yield ½ cup finely crushed peppermints. To crush, place unwrapped candy in a heavy-duty resealable food storage bag. Loosely seal the bag, leaving an opening for air to escape. Crush with a rolling pin, meat mallet or the bottom of a heavy skillet.

1. Place bittersweet and unsweetened chocolate in medium microwavable bowl. Microwave on HIGH at 30-second intervals, stirring between each interval until melted and smooth. Let stand 15 minutes.

2. Preheat oven to 325°F. Lightly grease or line cookie sheets with parchment paper.

3. Beat egg whites and salt in large bowl with electric mixer at high speed until soft peaks form. Gradually add sugar; beat 5 minutes or until stiff peaks form. Add chocolate; beat at low speed just until blended. Stir in peppermint extract, scraping down sides of bowl. Fold in coconut.

4. Shape dough by level tablespoonfuls into 1-inch balls; place 2 inches apart on prepared cookie sheets. Make small indentation in center. Sprinkle crushed candy into indentations.

5. Bake 12 minutes or until outside is crisp and inside is moist and chewy. Cool on cookie sheets 2 minutes. Remove to wire racks; cool completely.

Chocolate Almond Sandwiches

Makes about 2½ dozen sandwich cookies

1 package (about 16 ounces)
refrigerated sugar cookie
dough
4 ounces almond paste

¼ cup all-purpose flour
1 container (16 ounces) dark
chocolate frosting
Sliced almonds

1. Let dough stand at room temperature 15 minutes.

2. Beat dough, almond paste and flour in large bowl with electric mixer at medium speed until well blended. Divide dough into 3 pieces; freeze 20 minutes. Shape each piece into 10×1-inch log; wrap and refrigerate 2 hours or overnight. (Or freeze 1 hour or until firm.)

3. Preheat oven to 350°F. Lightly grease or line cookie sheets with parchment paper. Cut dough into ¼-inch slices; place 2 inches apart on prepared cookie sheets.

4. Bake 10 minutes or until edges are lightly browned. Cool on cookie sheets 2 minutes. Remove to wire racks; cool completely.

5. Spread frosting on flat sides of half of cookies; top with remaining cookies. Spread small amount of frosting on top of each sandwich cookie; top with 1 sliced almond.

Tip

Almond paste is a prepared product made of ground blanched almonds, sugar and an ingredient, such as glucose, glycerin or corn syrup, to keep it pliable. It is often used as an ingredient in confections and baked goods. Almond paste is available in cans and plastic tubes in most supermarkets or gourmet food markets. After opening, wrap the container tightly and store it in the refrigerator.

Decadent Coconut Macaroons

Makes about 3 dozen cookies

1 package (14 ounces) flaked
   coconut
¾ cup sugar
6 tablespoons all-purpose
   flour
¼ teaspoon salt

4 egg whites
1 teaspoon vanilla
1 cup (6 ounces) semisweet or
   bittersweet chocolate chips,
   melted

1. Preheat oven to 325°F. Lightly grease and flour or line cookie sheets with parchment paper.

2. Combine coconut, sugar, flour and salt in large bowl. Beat in egg whites and vanilla with electric mixer at medium speed until blended. Drop batter by tablespoonfuls 2 inches apart onto prepared cookie sheets.

3. Bake 20 minutes or until set and edges are lightly browned. Remove to wire racks; cool completely. Dip cookies in melted chocolate; let stand until set.

Espresso Cookie Cups

Makes 2 dozen cups

¼ cup (½ stick) unsalted butter
1 square (1 ounce)
  unsweetened chocolate,
  chopped
⅓ cup granulated sugar
2 tablespoons instant espresso
  powder
1 egg

1 teaspoon vanilla
2 tablespoons cake flour
¼ teaspoon salt
1 package (12 ounces) flaky
  honey-butter-flavored
  layered biscuits
Powdered sugar

1. Melt butter and chocolate in small heavy saucepan over low heat. Remove from heat; stir in granulated sugar and espresso powder. Whisk in egg and vanilla until blended. Stir in flour and salt.

2. Preheat oven to 350°F. Spray 24 mini (1¾-inch) muffin cups with nonstick cooking spray.

3. Separate individual biscuits, then pull each biscuit apart horizontally into 3 pieces each. Press each piece into bottom and up sides of muffin cups. Freeze 10 minutes.

4. Bake 6 minutes or until edges are lightly browned. While still warm, press bottom and sides of biscuits against pan with handle of wooden spoon to make well in center of cups. Fill centers with chocolate mixture.

5. Bake 7 minutes or until set. Remove to wire racks; cool completely. Dust with powdered sugar just before serving.

Tip

To easily dust cookies with powdered sugar, place a sheet of wax paper under the wire racks. Place powdered sugar in a small strainer and gently shake strainer over cooled cookies.

Linzer Sandwich Cookies

Makes about 2 dozen sandwich cookies

1⅔ cups all-purpose flour
¼ teaspoon baking powder
¼ teaspoon salt
¾ cup granulated sugar
½ cup (1 stick) butter, softened

1 egg
1 teaspoon vanilla
Seedless red raspberry jam
Powdered sugar

1. Whisk flour, baking powder and salt in small bowl. Beat granulated sugar and butter in medium bowl with electric mixer at medium speed until light and fluffy. Beat in egg and vanilla. Gradually add flour mixture, beating at low speed until dough forms. Divide dough in half; shape each half into disc. Wrap and refrigerate 2 hours or until firm.

2. Preheat oven to 375°F. Working with one disc at a time, roll out dough between sheets of parchment paper to ¼-inch thickness. Cut out shapes with fluted round cookie cutters. Cut out 1-inch centers from half of shapes. Place 1½ to 2 inches apart on ungreased cookie sheets. Repeat with trimmings.

3. Bake 8 minutes or until edges are lightly browned. Cool on cookie sheets 2 minutes. Remove to wire racks; cool completely.

4. Spread jam on flat sides of whole cookies, spreading almost to edges. Place cookies with cutouts over jam. Sprinkle cookies with powdered sugar.

Swedish Sandwich Cookies (Syltkakor)

Makes 1½ dozen sandwich cookies

1 cup (2 sticks) unsalted butter, softened

½ cup plus 2 tablespoons sugar, divided

2 egg yolks

2 to 2¼ cups all-purpose flour

3 tablespoons ground almonds

1 egg white

⅔ cup strawberry or red currant jelly

1. Beat butter and ½ cup sugar in large bowl with electric mixer at medium speed until light and fluffy. Beat in egg yolks until well blended. Gradually add 1½ cups flour, beating at low speed until blended. Stir in additional flour to form stiff dough. Divide dough in half; shape each half into disc. Wrap and refrigerate 2 hours or until firm.

2. Preheat oven to 375°F. Lightly grease and flour or line cookie sheets with parchment paper.

3. Roll out one disc of dough between sheets of parchment paper to ¼-inch thickness. Cut out shapes with 2¼-inch round cookie cutter. Place 1½ to 2 inches apart on prepared cookie sheets. Gently knead dough trimmings; reroll and cut out additional shapes.

4. Roll out remaining disc of dough between sheets of parchment paper to ¼-inch thickness. Cut out shapes with 2¼-inch fluted cookie cutter. Cut out 1-inch centers. Place 1½ to 2 inches apart on prepared cookie sheets. (Cut equal numbers of round and scalloped cookies.)

5. Combine almonds and remaining 2 tablespoons sugar in small bowl. Brush each fluted cookie with egg white; sprinkle with sugar mixture.

6. Bake 8 minutes or until set and lightly browned. Cool on cookie sheets 2 minutes. Remove cookies to wire racks; cool completely.

7. Spread jelly over flat sides of round cookies; top with fluted cookies.

Rosemary Honey Shortbread Cookies

Makes 2 dozen cookies

2 cups all-purpose flour
1 tablespoon fresh rosemary
  leaves,* minced
½ teaspoon salt
½ teaspoon baking powder
¾ cup (1½ sticks) unsalted
  butter, softened

½ cup powdered sugar
2 tablespoons honey

*For best flavor, use only fresh
rosemary or substitute fresh or dried
lavender buds.*

1. Whisk flour, rosemary, salt and baking powder in medium bowl. Beat butter, powdered sugar and honey in large bowl with electric mixer at medium speed until light and fluffy. Beat in flour mixture just until blended. (Mixture will be crumbly.)

2. Shape dough into 12-inch log. Wrap and refrigerate 1 hour or until firm. (Dough can be refrigerated several days before baking.)

3. Preheat oven to 350°F. Lightly grease or line cookie sheets with parchment paper. Cut log into ½-inch slices. Place 2 inches apart on prepared cookie sheets.

4. Bake 13 minutes or until set. Cool on cookie sheets 1 minute. Remove to wire racks; cool completely.

Chocolate Hazelnut Biscottini

Makes about 4½ dozen biscottini

2½ cups all-purpose flour

1 teaspoon baking powder

½ teaspoon salt

½ teaspoon ground cinnamon

¾ cup (1½ sticks) unsalted butter, softened

⅓ cup chocolate-hazelnut spread

¾ cup sugar

2 eggs

1 cup coarsely chopped toasted hazelnuts*

1 cup milk chocolate chips

*To toast hazelnuts, spread in single layer in medium skillet. Cook over medium heat 2 minutes, stirring frequently, or until skins begin to peel and nuts are lightly browned. Transfer to clean dish towel; rub hazelnuts to remove skins. Cool completely.

1. Whisk flour, baking powder, salt and cinnamon in medium bowl. Beat butter and chocolate-hazelnut spread in large bowl with electric mixer at medium speed until light and fluffy. Add sugar; beat until blended. Add eggs, one at a time, beating well after each addition. Add flour mixture, ½ cup at a time, beating well after each addition. Add hazelnuts and chocolate chips; stir just until blended.

2. Shape dough into two 13×2-inch logs; gently pat to smooth top. Refrigerate 3 to 4 hours.

3. Preheat oven to 350°F. Lightly grease baking sheet or line with parchment paper.

4. Bake 25 minutes or until set and lightly browned. Remove from oven. Cool on baking sheet 10 minutes.

5. *Reduce oven temperature to 325°F.* With serrated knife, cut each log into 1-inch-thick slices; cut each slice in half. Arrange slices on baking sheet.

6. Bake 15 minutes. Cool on baking sheet 5 minutes. Turn slices; bake 15 minutes. Cool completely on baking sheet on wire rack.

Chocolate Decadence

Deep Dark Chocolate Drops

Makes about 3 dozen cookies

1½ cups semisweet chocolate chips, divided
1¼ cups all-purpose flour
¼ cup unsweetened cocoa powder
½ teaspoon salt
½ teaspoon baking soda

½ cup granulated sugar
½ cup (1 stick) butter, softened
¼ cup packed brown sugar
1 egg
2 tablespoons milk
1 teaspoon vanilla

1. Preheat oven to 350°F. Lightly grease or line cookie sheets with parchment paper.

2. Place ½ cup chocolate chips in small microwavable bowl. Microwave on HIGH 1 minute; stir. Microwave at additional 30-second intervals, stirring after each interval until melted and smooth. Cool slightly.

3. Whisk flour, cocoa, salt and baking soda in medium bowl. Beat granulated sugar, butter and brown sugar in large bowl with electric mixer at medium speed until light and fluffy. Add egg, milk, vanilla and melted chocolate; beat until well blended. Add flour mixture; beat just until blended. Stir in remaining 1 cup chocolate chips.

4. Drop dough by rounded tablespoonfuls 2 inches apart onto prepared cookie sheets.

5. Bake 10 minutes or until set. Cool on cookie sheets 2 minutes. Remove to wire racks; cool completely.

Chocolate Pistachio Cookies

Makes about 3½ dozen cookies

2 cups shelled pistachio or macadamia nuts, finely chopped

1¾ cups all-purpose flour

¼ cup unsweetened cocoa powder

¾ teaspoon baking soda

½ teaspoon salt

¾ cup plus 1 tablespoon I CAN'T BELIEVE IT'S NOT BUTTER!® Spread

1 cup granulated sugar

¾ cup firmly packed brown sugar

2 eggs

3 squares (1 ounce each) unsweetened chocolate, melted

½ teaspoon vanilla extract

⅛ teaspoon almond extract

1½ squares (1 ounce each) unsweetened chocolate

2 tablespoons confectioners' sugar

Preheat oven to 375°F. Lightly spray baking sheets with I Can't Believe It's Not Butter! Spray; set aside. Reserve 3 tablespoons pistachios for garnish.

In medium bowl, combine flour, cocoa powder, baking soda and salt; set aside.

In large bowl with electric mixer, beat ¾ cup I Can't Believe It's Not Butter! Spread, granulated sugar and brown sugar until light and fluffy, about 5 minutes. Beat in eggs, one at a time, beating 30 seconds after each addition. Beat in melted chocolate and extracts. Beat in flour mixture just until blended. Stir in pistachios.

On prepared baking sheets, drop dough by rounded tablespoonfuls 1 inch apart. Bake, one sheet at a time, 8 minutes or until tops are puffed and dry but still soft when touched. Do not overbake. On wire rack, cool 5 minutes; remove from sheets and cool completely.

For icing, in microwave-safe bowl, melt 1½ squares chocolate with remaining 1 tablespoon I Can't Believe It's Not Butter! Spread at HIGH (100%) 1 minute or until chocolate is melted; stir until smooth. Stir in confectioners' sugar. Lightly spread ¼ teaspoon icing on each cookie, then sprinkle with reserved pistachios. Let stand 20 minutes before serving.

Cocoa Crackles

Makes about 3½ dozen cookies

1½ cups all-purpose flour
⅓ cup unsweetened cocoa
   powder
½ teaspoon salt
½ teaspoon baking soda
½ cup granulated sugar

½ cup (1 stick) butter, softened
¼ cup packed light brown
   sugar
2 eggs
1 teaspoon vanilla
Powdered sugar

1. Preheat oven to 350°F. Lightly grease or line cookie sheets with parchment paper.

2. Combine flour, cocoa, salt and baking soda in medium bowl. Beat granulated sugar, butter and brown sugar in large bowl with electric mixer at medium speed until light and fluffy. Add eggs and vanilla; beat until well blended. Add flour mixture; beat just until blended.

3. Place powdered sugar in shallow bowl. Shape heaping teaspoonfuls of dough into balls. Roll in powdered sugar; place 2 inches apart on prepared cookie sheets.

4. Bake 11 minutes or until set and no longer shiny. Cool on cookie sheets 2 minutes. Remove to wire racks; cool completely.

Chocolate Pinwheels

Makes about 3½ dozen cookies

2 cups (4 sticks) unsalted
butter, softened
1 cup powdered sugar
¼ cup packed light brown
sugar
½ teaspoon salt

4 cups all-purpose flour
½ cup semisweet chocolate
chips, melted
1 tablespoon unsweetened
cocoa

1. Beat butter, powdered sugar, brown sugar and salt in large bowl with electric mixer at medium speed 2 minutes or until light and fluffy. Gradually add flour, beating until well blended.

2. Divide dough in half; set one half aside. Add melted chocolate and cocoa to remaining dough; beat until well blended.

3. Shape chocolate and plain doughs into 4 balls each. Roll out 1 ball plain dough between sheets of parchment paper to 12×6-inch rectangle. Roll out 1 ball chocolate dough between sheets of parchment paper to 12×6-inch rectangle; place over plain dough. Starting at wide end, tightly roll up jelly-roll style to form 12-inch log. If dough crumbles or breaks, press back together and continue to roll (the effect will be marbled, not spiralled, but just as attractive). Wrap and refrigerate 1 hour. Repeat with remaining dough.

4. Preheat oven to 300°F. Cut each log into 20 slices; place 2 inches apart on ungreased cookie sheets.

5. Bake 13 minutes or until set and lightly browned. Cool on cookie sheets 5 minutes. Remove to wire racks; cool completely.

Mint Chocolate Delights

Makes 2 dozen sandwich cookies

1 cup (2 sticks) unsalted butter, softened, divided

½ cup granulated sugar

⅓ cup packed dark brown sugar

⅓ cup semisweet chocolate chips, melted and slightly cooled

1 egg

½ teaspoon vanilla

1½ cups all-purpose flour

¼ cup unsweetened cocoa powder

½ teaspoon salt, divided

2½ cups powdered sugar

½ teaspoon mint extract

3 to 4 drops red food coloring

2 to 3 tablespoons milk or half-and-half

1. Beat ½ cup butter, granulated sugar and brown sugar in large bowl with electric mixer at medium speed until light and fluffy. Add melted chocolate, egg and vanilla; beat until well blended.

2. Whisk flour, cocoa and ¼ teaspoon salt in small bowl. Gradually add to butter mixture, beating well after each addition. Shape dough into 16-inch log. Wrap and refrigerate 1 hour or until firm.

3. Preheat oven to 400°F. Lightly grease or line cookie sheets with parchment paper. Cut log into ¼-inch slices. Place 2 inches apart on prepared cookie sheets.

4. Bake 10 minutes or until set. Cool on cookie sheets 5 minutes. Remove to wire racks; cool completely.

5. Beat powdered sugar, remaining ½ cup butter and ¼ teaspoon salt in large bowl with electric mixer at medium speed until well blended. Add mint extract and food coloring; beat until well blended. Beat in milk, 1 tablespoon at a time, until light and fluffy. Spread filling on flat sides of half of cookies; top with remaining cookies.

Mocha Dots

Makes about 6½ dozen cookies

1 tablespoon instant coffee
  granules
2 tablespoons hot water
1½ cups all-purpose flour
¼ cup unsweetened cocoa
  powder
½ teaspoon salt
½ teaspoon baking soda
½ cup granulated sugar

½ cup (1 stick) butter, softened
¼ cup packed light brown
  sugar
1 egg
1 teaspoon vanilla
  Chocolate nonpareil
  candies (about 1 inch in
  diameter)

1. Preheat oven to 350°F. Lightly grease or line cookie sheets with parchment paper.

2. Dissolve instant coffee granules in hot water in small bowl; cool slightly. Whisk flour, cocoa, salt and baking soda in medium bowl.

3. Beat granulated sugar, butter and brown sugar in large bowl with electric mixer at medium speed until light and fluffy. Add coffee mixture, egg and vanilla; beat until well blended. Add flour mixture; beat until well blended.

4. Shape dough by level teaspoonfuls into balls; place 2 inches apart on prepared cookie sheets. Gently press 1 candy onto center of each ball. (Do not press candies too far into dough balls. Cookies will spread around candies as they bake.)

5. Bake 8 minutes or until set and no longer shiny. Cool on cookie sheets 2 minutes. Remove to wire racks; cool completely.

Dark Cocoa Spice Cookies

Makes about 5 dozen cookies

2½ cups all-purpose flour
½ cup unsweetened Dutch
 process cocoa powder
1 teaspoon ground cinnamon
1 teaspoon ground
 cardamom
½ teaspoon baking soda
¼ teaspoon salt
1½ cups packed dark brown
 sugar

1 cup (2 sticks) unsalted
 butter, softened
2 egg yolks
1 teaspoon coconut extract
1¼ cups sifted powdered sugar
1 egg white
 Pinch cream of tartar
 Decorating sugar or
 demerara sugar

1. Sift flour, cocoa, cinnamon, cardamom, baking soda and salt into medium bowl.

2. Beat brown sugar and butter in large bowl with electric mixer at medium speed until light and fluffy. Beat in egg yolks and coconut extract. Add flour mixture; beat until blended.

3. Gather dough into ball and divide into 4 equal pieces. Shape each piece into 6-inch log. Wrap and refrigerate 4 hours or overnight.

4. Preheat oven to 325°F. Lightly grease or line cookie sheets with parchment paper. Cut each log into 16 slices. Place 1 inch apart on prepared cookie sheets.

5. Bake 12 minutes or until set. Cool on cookie sheets 5 minutes. Remove to wire racks; cool completely.

6. Beat powdered sugar, egg white and cream of tartar in small bowl with electric mixer at medium speed until thick and smooth. Cover with damp cloth during use to prevent icing from drying out. Use small paintbrush to brush edges of cooled cookies with icing, then roll edges in sugar before icing hardens.

Mini Chocolate Whoopie Pies

Makes about 2 dozen sandwich cookies

1¾ cups all-purpose flour
½ cup unsweetened Dutch
    process cocoa powder
¾ teaspoon baking powder
½ teaspoon baking soda
½ teaspoon salt
1 cup packed brown sugar

1 cup (2 sticks) butter,
    softened, divided
1 egg
1½ teaspoons vanilla, divided
1 cup milk
1 cup powdered sugar
1 cup marshmallow creme

1. Preheat oven to 350°F. Lightly grease or line cookie sheets with parchment paper.

2. Sift flour, cocoa, baking powder, baking soda and salt into medium bowl. Beat brown sugar and ½ cup butter in large bowl with electric mixer at medium-high speed until light and fluffy. Beat in egg and 1 teaspoon vanilla until well blended. Alternately add flour mixture and milk, beating at low speed until smooth and well blended after each addition. Drop dough by heaping teaspoonfuls 2 inches apart onto prepared cookie sheets.

3. Bake 8 minutes or until cookies are puffed and tops spring back when lightly touched. Cool on cookie sheets 10 minutes. Remove to wire racks; cool completely.

4. Meanwhile, beat remaining ½ cup butter, ½ teaspoon vanilla, powdered sugar and marshmallow creme in large bowl at high speed 2 minutes or until light and fluffy.

5. Spoon heaping teaspoon filling onto flat side of half of cookies; top with remaining cookies.

Chocolate-Frosted Marshmallow Cookies

Makes about 5 dozen cookies

¾ cup (1½ sticks) butter, divided

3½ squares (1 ounce each) unsweetened chocolate, divided

1 cup packed brown sugar

1 egg

2 teaspoons vanilla, divided

½ teaspoon baking soda

1½ cups all-purpose flour

½ cup milk

1 package (16 ounces) marshmallows, halved crosswise

1½ cups powdered sugar

1 egg white

1. Preheat oven to 350°F. Lightly grease or line cookie sheets with parchment paper.

2. Melt ½ cup butter and 2 squares chocolate in small heavy saucepan over low heat, stirring until smooth. Remove from heat; cool slightly.

3. Beat brown sugar, egg, 1 teaspoon vanilla and baking soda in large bowl with electric mixer at medium speed until light and fluffy. Beat in chocolate mixture and flour until smooth. Beat in milk at low speed until blended. Drop dough by teaspoonfuls 2 inches apart onto prepared cookie sheets.

4. Bake 10 minutes or until set. Immediately place marshmallow half, cut side down, on each baked cookie. Bake 1 minute or just until marshmallow is warm enough to stick to cookie. Remove to wire racks; cool completely.

5. Melt remaining ¼ cup butter and 1½ squares chocolate in small heavy saucepan over low heat, stirring until smooth. Beat in powdered sugar until well blended. Beat in egg white and remaining 1 teaspoon vanilla, adding a little water, if necessary, to make smooth, slightly soft frosting. Spoon frosting over cookies to cover marshmallows.

Chocolate Cherry Cookies

Makes about 4 dozen cookies

1 package (about 18 ounces) devil's food cake mix
¾ cup (1½ sticks) butter, softened
2 eggs

1 teaspoon almond extract
24 maraschino cherries, rinsed, drained and cut into halves
¼ cup white chocolate chips
1 teaspoon canola oil

1. Preheat oven to 350°F. Lightly grease or line cookie sheets with parchment paper.

2. Beat cake mix, butter, eggs and almond extract in medium bowl with electric mixer at low speed until crumbly. Beat at medium speed 2 minutes or until smooth dough forms. (Dough will be very sticky.)

3. Shape dough into 1-inch balls. Place 2½ inches apart on prepared cookie sheets; flatten slightly. Place 1 cherry half in center of each cookie.

4. Bake 8 to 9 minutes or until cookies are no longer shiny and tops begin to crack. Cool on cookie sheets 2 minutes. Remove to wire racks; cool completely.

5. Place white chocolate chips and oil in small microwavable bowl. Microwave on HIGH 30 seconds. Repeat, stirring at 30-second intervals, until chocolate is melted and mixture is smooth. Drizzle over cookies. Let stand until set.

Kiddie Creations

Monogram Cookies

Makes 2 dozen cookies

3½ cups all-purpose flour
1 teaspoon salt
1½ cups sugar
1 cup (2 sticks) unsalted
    butter, softened
2 eggs

2 teaspoons vanilla
  Gel food coloring
1 container (16 ounces) white
    or vanilla frosting
  Assorted jumbo nonpareils
    (optional)

1. Whisk flour and salt in medium bowl. Beat sugar and butter in large bowl with electric mixer at medium speed until light and fluffy. Add eggs, one at a time, beating well after each addition. Add vanilla; beat until blended.

2. Gradually add flour mixture, beating well after each addition. Divide dough in half; shape each half into disc. Wrap and refrigerate 1 hour.

3. Preheat oven to 350°F. Lightly grease or line cookie sheets with parchment paper.

4. Working with one disc at a time, roll out dough between sheets of parchment paper to ¼-inch thickness. Cut out circles with 3-inch fluted round cookie cutter. Place 1 inch apart on prepared cookie sheets. Cut out letters using 1-inch alphabet cookie cutters; discard. Refrigerate 15 minutes.

5. Bake 15 minutes or until set. Cool on cookie sheets 5 minutes. Remove to wire racks; cool completely.

6. Add food coloring, a few drops at a time, to frosting; stir until evenly tinted. Spread cookies with frosting. Decorate with nonpareils, if desired. Let stand 10 minutes or until set.

Mischievous Monkeys

Makes 10 cookies

3 cups all-purpose flour
½ cup unsweetened cocoa
  powder
1 teaspoon salt
1½ cups sugar
1 cup (2 sticks) unsalted
  butter, softened
2 eggs

1 teaspoon vanilla
  Yellow gel food coloring
1 cup prepared white or
  vanilla frosting
  Black string licorice
20 brown candy-coated peanut
  butter candies

1. Whisk flour, cocoa and salt in medium bowl. Beat sugar and butter in large bowl with electric mixer at medium speed until light and fluffy. Add eggs, one at a time, beating well after each addition. Add vanilla; beat until blended.

2. Gradually add flour mixture, beating well after each addition. Divide dough in half; shape each half into disc. Wrap and refrigerate 1 hour.

3. Preheat oven to 350°F. Lightly grease or line cookie sheets with parchment paper.

4. Working with one disc at a time, roll out dough between sheets of parchment paper to ¼-inch thickness. From each disc, cut out 5 large circles with 3-inch round cookie cutter, 5 medium circles with 2-inch round cookie cutter and 10 small circles with 1½-inch round cookie cutter.

5. Place large circles 3 inches apart on prepared cookie sheets. Place 2 small circles next to each large circle for ears. Place medium circles 1 inch apart on separate prepared cookie sheet. Refrigerate 15 minutes.

6. Bake circles 12 minutes or until set. Cool on cookie sheets 5 minutes. Remove to wire racks; cool completely.

7. Add food coloring, a few drops at a time, to frosting; stir until evenly tinted. Spread medium circles with frosting. Let stand 10 minutes or until set. Spread thin layer of frosting on backs of medium circles and adhere to large circles for mouth. Cut lengths of licorice for noses and mouths; press into frosting.

8. Spread small circle of frosting on inside of each small circle for ears. Dot backs of 2 candies with frosting; adhere to each large circle just above medium circle for eyes. Let stand 10 minutes or until set.

Makin' Bacon Cookies

Makes about 2 dozen cookies

1 package (about 16 ounces) refrigerated break-apart sugar cookie dough (24 count)

½ cup water, divided
Red, brown and yellow gel food colorings

1. Let dough stand at room temperature 5 minutes. Lightly grease or line cookie sheets with parchment paper.

2. Preheat oven to 325°F. Roll out dough between sheets of parchment paper to ¼-inch thickness. Cut out bacon shapes with sharp knife (approximately 3½×1-inch shapes). Place 2 inches apart on prepared cookie sheets. Refrigerate 15 minutes.

3. Bake 13 minutes or until set. Cool on cookie sheets 5 minutes. Remove to wire racks; cool completely.

4. Place ¼ cup water in small bowl. Add red and brown food colorings, a few drops at a time; stir until evenly tinted. Place remaining ¼ cup water in another small bowl. Add red and yellow food colorings, a few drops at a time; stir until evenly tinted. Paint cookies to resemble bacon with small clean paintbrushes,* using as little water as possible for color to saturate. Leave some areas unpainted to resemble bacon fat. Let stand 1 hour or until dry.

Do not use paintbrushes that have been used for anything other than food.

Tip

To make your own custom-designed cutout cookies, cut a simple bacon shape out of clean, heavy cardboard or poster board. Place the cardboard pattern on the rolled out cookie dough and cut around it using a sharp knife.

Snapshot Cookies

Makes 1 dozen cookies

3½ cups all-purpose flour
1 teaspoon salt
1½ cups sugar
1 cup (2 sticks) unsalted butter, softened
2 eggs

2 teaspoons vanilla
Royal Icing (recipe follows)
Black gel food coloring
Assorted colored round candies
12 mini gummy candies

1. Whisk flour and salt in medium bowl. Beat sugar and butter in large bowl with electric mixer at medium speed until light and fluffy. Add eggs, one at a time, beating well after each addition. Add vanilla; beat until blended.

2. Gradually add flour mixture, beating well after each addition. Divide dough in half; shape into discs. Wrap and refrigerate 1 hour or until chilled.

3. Preheat oven to 350°F. Lightly grease or line cookie sheets with parchment paper.

4. Working with one disc at a time, roll out dough between sheets of parchment paper to ¼-inch thickness. From each disc, cut out 6 rectangles with sharp knife (approximately 2½×3½-inch shapes) and 6 circles with 1½-inch round cookie cutter.

5. Place rectangles 2 inches apart on prepared cookie sheets. Place circles 1 inch apart on separate prepared cookie sheet. Refrigerate 15 minutes.

6. Bake rectangles 15 minutes or until set. Bake circles 12 minutes or until set. Cool on cookie sheets 5 minutes. Remove to wire racks; cool completely.

7. Prepare Royal Icing. Reserve 1 cup Royal Icing. Add food coloring, a few drops at a time, to remaining icing; stir until evenly tinted. Spread rectangles with black icing. Let stand 10 minutes or until set. Spread circles with reserved white icing. Spread thin layer of white icing on back of circles and adhere to rectangles for lens. Let stand 10 minutes or until set.

8. Dot back of candies with icing and adhere for flash, viewfinder and lens. Dot back of gummy candy with icing and adhere to side of rectangle for button. Let stand 10 minutes or until set.

Royal Icing: Combine 4 cups powdered sugar, ¼ cup plus 2 tablespoons water and 3 tablespoons meringue powder in medium bowl. Beat with electric mixer at high speed 7 minutes or until soft peaks form. Cover surface with plastic wrap until needed. Makes about 2 cups.

Mighty Milk Shakes

Makes 1½ dozen brownies

1 package (about 19 ounces) brownie mix, plus ingredients to prepare mix

1 package (14 ounces) milk chocolate or peanut butter candy discs

½ (16-ounce) container white or vanilla frosting

Colored drinking straws

Colored sprinkles

1. Preheat oven to 350°F. Coat 9-inch square baking pan with nonstick cooking spray.

2. Prepare brownie mix according to package directions; pour batter into prepared pan. Bake 35 minutes or until toothpick inserted into center comes out clean. Cool completely in pan on wire rack. Cover; freeze 1 hour or overnight.

3. Run knife around edges of brownies. Place cutting board over baking pan; invert and let stand until brownies release from pan. Trim edges; discard. Cut into 18 rectangles.

4. Place candy discs in medium microwavable bowl. Microwave on HIGH 1 minute; stir. If necessary, microwave at additional 15-second intervals until smooth and spreadable. Stand brownies up on small side. Spread all sides with candy mixture. Let stand on wire racks 10 minutes or until set.

5. Pipe frosting on top of each brownie for whipped cream. Decorate with straws and sprinkles.

Building Blocks

Makes about 2½ dozen cookies

1 package (about 16 ounces) refrigerated cookie dough, any flavor	Assorted food colorings
Powdered Sugar Glaze (recipe follows)	Assorted small round gummy candies (about ¼ inch in diameter)

1. Let dough stand at room temperature 15 minutes. Grease 13×9-inch baking pan.

2. Preheat oven to 350°F. Press dough evenly into bottom of prepared pan. Score dough lengthwise and crosswise into 32 equal rectangles (about 2¼×1½ inches each). Freeze 10 minutes.

3. Bake 10 minutes. Re-score partially baked cookies. Bake 5 minutes or until edges are lightly browned and center is set. Cut through score marks to separate cookies. Cool in pan 10 minutes. Remove to wire racks; cool completely.

4. Prepare Powdered Sugar Glaze. Tint glaze with food colorings as desired.

5. Place wire racks over waxed paper. Spread glaze over tops and sides of cookies. Let stand 5 minutes. Attach 6 gummy candies to each cookie. Let stand 40 minutes or until set.

Powdered Sugar Glaze

Makes about 1 cup glaze

2 cups powdered sugar	1 teaspoon vanilla
6 to 9 tablespoons whipping cream, divided	

Combine powdered sugar, 6 tablespoons cream and vanilla in medium bowl; whisk until smooth. Add enough remaining cream, 1 tablespoon at a time, to make pourable glaze.

Snickerpoodles

Makes about 2 dozen cookies

1 package (about 16 ounces) refrigerated sugar cookie dough

1 teaspoon ground cinnamon, divided

1 teaspoon vanilla

¼ cup sugar

Semisweet chocolate chips

Mini semisweet chocolate chips

White and pink decorating icings

1. Let dough stand at room temperature 15 minutes. Lightly grease or line cookie sheets with parchment paper.

2. Preheat oven to 350°F. Combine dough, ½ teaspoon cinnamon and vanilla in large bowl; beat with electric mixer at medium speed until well blended. Combine sugar and remaining ½ teaspoon cinnamon in small bowl.

3. Shape 1½ teaspoonfuls dough into oval for face. Roll in cinnamon-sugar; place on prepared cookie sheets. Divide 1½ teaspoonfuls dough in half; shape each half into teardrop shape. Roll in cinnamon-sugar; place at either side of face. Shape scant teaspoonful dough into oval. Roll in cinnamon-sugar; place at top of face. Repeat with remaining dough and cinnamon-sugar.

4. Bake 10 minutes or until edges are lightly browned. Immediately press 1 chocolate chip onto each face for nose. Cool on cookie sheets 2 minutes. Remove to wire racks; cool completely.

5. Pipe two small circles on each face with white decorating icing. Press mini chocolate chips into icing for eyes. Decorate as desired with white and pink icings.

Holiday Delights

Window-to-My-Heart Cookies

Makes about 3 dozen cookies

2¼ cups all-purpose flour
½ teaspoon salt
¼ teaspoon baking powder
1 cup (2 sticks) butter, softened
½ cup powdered sugar
¼ cup packed brown sugar

1 teaspoon vanilla
1 cup dried cranberries, chopped
15 to 20 cherry- or cinnamon-flavored hard candies, crushed

1. Whisk flour, salt and baking powder in medium bowl. Beat butter, powdered sugar, brown sugar and vanilla in large bowl with electric mixer at medium speed until light and fluffy. Gradually add flour mixture, beating well after each addition. Stir in cranberries. Shape dough into disc. Wrap and refrigerate 1 hour.

2. Preheat oven to 325°F. Lightly grease or line cookie sheets with parchment paper.

3. Roll out dough between sheets of parchment paper to ¼-inch thickness. Cut out shapes using 2- to 3-inch heart cookie cutter. Cut out center of each cookie using smaller heart cookie cutter; re-roll scraps to make additional hearts. Place 1 inch apart on prepared cookie sheets. Sprinkle crushed candy into each center.

4. Bake 20 minutes or until candy is melted and cookies are set. Remove to wire racks; cool completely.

Snowpeople Cookies

Makes 1 dozen cookies

2¼ cups all-purpose flour
½ teaspoon baking soda
1 package (8 ounces) cream
  cheese, softened
1 cup powdered sugar
½ cup (1 stick) unsalted butter,
  softened
½ teaspoon almond extract

Additional powdered sugar
12 sticks red or striped
  chewing gum
Mini candy-coated
  chocolate pieces
Red gummy candies,
  flattened and trimmed
Decorating icing

1. Preheat oven to 325°F. Lightly grease or line cookie sheets with parchment paper.

2. Whisk flour and baking soda in medium bowl. Beat cream cheese, 1 cup powdered sugar, butter and almond extract in large bowl with electric mixer at medium speed until well blended.

3. Shape dough into equal number of ½-inch, 1-inch and 1½-inch diameter balls. Using one small, medium and large ball per snowperson, place balls nearly touching on prepared cookie sheets. Flatten each ball to ¼-inch thickness using bottom of glass dipped in flour.

4. Bake 15 minutes or until edges are lightly browned. Cool on cookie sheets 1 minute. Remove to wire racks; cool completely.

5. Sprinkle each snowperson with additional powdered sugar. Using 1 stick of gum, make scarf with fringed ends for each snowperson. Use chocolate pieces for eyes and gummy candies for mouths, securing with decorating icing.

Christmas Clouds

Makes 2½ dozen cookies

2 cups all-purpose flour
1 cup finely chopped pecans
1 teaspoon ground cinnamon
1 cup (2 sticks) unsalted
    butter, softened

1 cup powdered sugar,
    divided
1 teaspoon vanilla

1. Preheat oven to 350°F.

2. Combine flour, pecans and cinnamon in medium bowl. Beat butter, ½ cup powdered sugar and vanilla in large bowl with electric mixer at medium speed until light and fluffy. Gradually add flour mixture, beating at low speed until blended after each addition. (Dough will be stiff and crumbly.)

3. Shape dough by tablespoonfuls into 1-inch balls; place 2 inches apart on ungreased cookie sheets.

4. Bake 15 minutes or until bottoms are lightly browned. Cool on cookie sheets 5 minutes. Gently roll warm cookies in remaining ½ cup powdered sugar. Remove to wire racks; cool completely.

Peppermint Snowballs

Makes 2 dozen snowballs

1½ cups sweetened shredded coconut

½ cup finely crushed peppermint candies*

¼ cup (½ stick) unsalted butter

4 cups mini marshmallows

½ teaspoon peppermint extract (optional)

5 cups crispy rice breakfast cereal

Vegetable oil

*About 18 peppermint candies will yield ½ cup finely crushed peppermints. To crush, place unwrapped candy in a heavy-duty resealable food storage bag. Loosely seal the bag, leaving an opening for air to escape. Crush with a rolling pin, meat mallet or the bottom of a heavy skillet.

1. Combine coconut and crushed candies in shallow pan.

2. Melt butter in large heavy saucepan over low heat. Add marshmallows; cook and stir until melted. Remove from heat. (Or place butter and marshmallows in large microwavable bowl. Microwave on HIGH at 30-second intervals, stirring between each interval until melted and smooth.)

3. While mixture is still warm, gently mix in peppermint extract, if desired, and rice cereal, stirring until well coated. With lightly oiled fingers, shape mixture into 24 (2-inch) balls. Roll balls in coconut mixture. Let stand until cool.

Tip

Snowballs can be frozen in resealable food storage bags or layered in an airtight container between sheets of waxed paper.

Buttery Almond Cutouts

Makes about 3 dozen cookies

1½ cups granulated sugar
1 cup (2 sticks) butter, softened
¾ cup sour cream
2 eggs
3 teaspoons almond extract, divided
1 teaspoon vanilla
4⅓ cups all-purpose flour
1 teaspoon baking powder

1 teaspoon baking soda
½ teaspoon salt
2 cups powdered sugar
2 tablespoons milk
1 tablespoon light corn syrup
Assorted food coloring, decorating gels, decorating sugars, sprinkles and decors

1. Beat granulated sugar and butter in large bowl with electric mixer at medium speed until light and fluffy. Add sour cream, eggs, 2 teaspoons almond extract and vanilla; beat until smooth. Add flour, baking powder, baking soda and salt; beat until well blended. Divide dough into four pieces; shape each piece into disc. Wrap each disc tightly with plastic wrap. Refrigerate at least 3 hours or up to 3 days.

2. Combine powdered sugar, milk, corn syrup and remaining 1 teaspoon almond extract in small bowl; stir until smooth. Cover and refrigerate until ready to use or up to 3 days.

3. Preheat oven to 375°F. Working with one disc of dough at a time, roll out on floured surface to ¼-inch thickness. Cut out shapes using 2½-inch cookie cutters. Place cutouts 2 inches apart on ungreased cookie sheets. Bake 7 to 8 minutes or until edges are set and lightly browned. Remove to wire racks; cool completely.

4. Divide powdered sugar mixture among three or four small bowls; tint each with desired food coloring. Frost and decorate cookies as desired; let stand until set.

Note: To freeze dough, place wrapped discs in large resealable food storage bags. Thaw at room temperature before using. Or, cut out dough, bake and cool cookies completely. Freeze unglazed cookies for up to 2 months. Thaw and glaze as desired.

Hanukkah Cookies

Makes 3½ dozen cookies

½ cup (1 stick) unsalted butter, softened
½ cup sugar
1 package (3 ounces) cream cheese, softened
¼ cup honey
1 egg

½ teaspoon vanilla
2½ cups all-purpose flour
⅓ cup finely ground walnuts
1 teaspoon baking powder
¼ teaspoon salt
Blue, white and yellow decorating icings

1. Beat butter, sugar, cream cheese, honey, egg and vanilla in large bowl with electric mixer at medium speed until light and fluffy. Stir in flour, walnuts, baking powder and salt until well blended. Divide dough in half; shape each half into disc. Wrap and refrigerate 2 hours or until firm.

2. Preheat oven to 350°F. Lightly grease or line cookie sheets with parchment paper.

3. Working with one disc at a time, roll out dough between sheets of parchment paper to ¼-inch thickness. Cut out shapes with 2½-inch dreidel and 6-pointed star cookie cutters. Place 2 inches apart on prepared cookie sheets.

4. Bake 8 minutes or until edges are lightly browned. Cool on cookie sheets 2 minutes. Remove to wire racks; cool completely. Decorate as desired with blue, white and yellow icings.

Tip

Unbaked cookie dough can be refrigerated for up to 2 weeks or frozen for up to 6 weeks. Label the dough with baking information for added convenience.

Buche de Noel Cookies

Makes about 2½ dozen cookies

⅔ cup butter or margarine, softened
1 cup granulated sugar
2 eggs
2 teaspoons vanilla extract
2½ cups all-purpose flour

½ cup HERSHEY'S® Cocoa
½ teaspoon baking soda
¼ teaspoon salt
Mocha Frosting (recipe follows)
Powdered sugar (optional)

1. Beat butter and granulated sugar with electric mixer on medium speed in large bowl until well blended. Add eggs and vanilla; beat until fluffy. Stir together flour, cocoa, baking soda and salt; gradually add to butter mixture, beating until well blended. Cover; refrigerate dough 1 to 2 hours.

2. Heat oven to 350°F. Shape heaping teaspoons of dough into logs about 2½ inches long and ¾ inches in diameter; place on ungreased cookie sheet. Bake 7 to 9 minutes or until set. Cool slightly. Remove to wire rack and cool completely.

3. Frost cookies with Mocha Frosting. Using tines of fork, draw lines through frosting to imitate tree bark. Lightly dust with powdered sugar, if desired.

Mocha Frosting

Makes about 1⅔ cups frosting

6 tablespoons butter or margarine, softened
2⅔ cups powdered sugar
⅓ cup HERSHEY'S® Cocoa
3 to 4 tablespoons milk

2 teaspoons powdered instant espresso powder dissolved in 1 teaspoon hot water
1 teaspoon vanilla extract

Beat butter with electric mixer on medium speed in medium bowl until creamy. Add powdered sugar and cocoa alternately with milk, dissolved espresso and vanilla, beating to spreadable consistency.

Jolly Peanut Butter Gingerbread Cookies

Makes about 6 dozen cookies

1⅔ cups (10-ounce package) REESE'S® Peanut Butter Chips
¾ cup (1½ sticks) butter or margarine, softened
1 cup packed light brown sugar
1 cup dark corn syrup

2 eggs
5 cups all-purpose flour
1 teaspoon baking soda
½ teaspoon ground cinnamon
¼ teaspoon ground ginger
¼ teaspoon salt

1. Place peanut butter chips in small microwave-safe bowl. Microwave at MEDIUM (50%) 1 minute; stir. If necessary, microwave at MEDIUM an additional 15 seconds at a time, stirring after each heating, until chips are melted when stirred. Beat melted peanut butter chips and butter in large bowl until well blended. Add brown sugar, corn syrup and eggs; beat until fluffy.

2. Stir together flour, baking soda, cinnamon, ginger and salt. Add half of flour mixture to butter mixture; beat on low speed of mixer until smooth. With wooden spoon, stir in remaining flour mixture until well blended. Divide into thirds; wrap each in plastic wrap. Refrigerate at least 1 hour or until dough is firm enough to roll.

3. Heat oven to 325°F. On lightly floured surface, roll 1 dough portion at a time to ⅛-inch thickness; cut into holiday shapes with floured cookie cutters. Place on ungreased cookie sheet.

4. Bake 10 to 12 minutes or until set and lightly browned. Cool slightly; remove from cookie sheet to wire rack. Cool completely. Frost and decorate as desired.

Festive Candy Canes

Makes about 2 dozen cookies

1 cup powdered sugar
¾ cup (1½ sticks) butter, softened
1 egg
1 teaspoon peppermint extract

½ teaspoon vanilla
1⅔ to 1¾ cups all-purpose flour
⅛ teaspoon salt
Red food coloring

1. Preheat oven to 350°F.

2. Beat powdered sugar and butter in large bowl with electric mixer at medium speed until light and fluffy. Add egg, peppermint extract and vanilla; beat until well blended. Add flour and salt; beat until well blended. (Dough will be sticky.)

3. Divide dough in half. Add red food coloring to half of dough, a few drops at a time; knead until evenly tinted. Leave remaining dough plain. For each candy cane, shape heaping teaspoonful of each color dough into 5-inch rope with floured hands. Twist together into candy cane shape. Place 2 inches apart on ungreased cookie sheets.

4. Bake 8 minutes or until set and edges are lightly browned. Cool on cookie sheets 2 minutes. Remove to wire racks; cool completely.

Bar Cookie Bonanza

Autumn Pumpkin Bars

Makes about 1½ dozen bars

2 cups all-purpose flour
2 teaspoons pumpkin pie
   spice
1 teaspoon baking powder
½ teaspoon salt
¼ teaspoon baking soda
1 cup plus 2 tablespoons
   packed brown sugar

¾ cup (1½ sticks) butter,
   softened
1 egg
1½ cups solid-pack pumpkin
1 teaspoon vanilla
1 cup semisweet chocolate
   chips, melted

1. Preheat oven to 350°F. Grease 13×9-inch baking pan.

2. Whisk flour, pumpkin pie spice, baking powder, salt and baking soda in medium bowl. Beat brown sugar and butter in large bowl with electric mixer at medium speed 3 minutes or until light and fluffy. Beat in egg until blended. Beat in pumpkin and vanilla. (Mixture may look curdled.)

3. Gradually add flour mixture, beating at low speed just until blended after each addition. Spread batter evenly in prepared pan.

4. Bake 25 minutes or until toothpick inserted into center comes out clean. Cool completely in pan on wire rack.

5. Cut out pumpkin and leaf shapes with 2- to 3-inch cookie cutters. Place melted chocolate in small resealable food storage bag. Cut off small corner. Pipe veins on leaves and lines on pumpkins with chocolate.

Apricot Almond Bars

Makes 3 dozen bars

½ cup (1 stick) plus
2 tablespoons butter

⅓ cup granulated sugar

¾ teaspoon almond extract, divided

1½ cups all-purpose flour

⅛ teaspoon salt

½ cup apricot or any flavor preserves

½ cup powdered sugar

2 to 2½ teaspoons fresh lemon juice or water

¼ cup toasted almonds* (optional)

To toast almonds, spread sliced almonds in a shallow pan. Bake at 350°F for about 5 minutes or until lightly browned. Almonds burn easily.

Beat butter, sugar and ½ teaspoon almond extract with an electric mixer until fluffy. Stir in flour and salt. Dough will be stiff. Divide into 4 sections. Roll each section into a 9-inch log. Space at least 3 inches apart on cookie sheet. Using side of finger or handle of a wooden spoon, make a groove down center of each log about halfway into the log.

Bake in 375°F preheated oven for 10 minutes. Remove from oven and fill the groove with preserves. Return to oven and bake an additional 6 to 8 minutes or until golden.

Combine powdered sugar, ¼ teaspoon almond extract and enough lemon juice or water to make a frosting that can be drizzled. Drizzle frosting over preserves while bars are still warm. Sprinkle immediately with almonds. Cut into 1-inch bars with a sharp knife.

Favorite recipe from **North Dakota Wheat Commission**

Holiday Walnut Berry Bites

Makes 4 dozen bars

Cooking spray
2½ cups all-purpose flour
1 cup (2 sticks) cold
   margarine, cut into pieces
½ cup confectioners' sugar
½ teaspoon salt
1⅓ cups KARO® Light Corn
   Syrup

4 eggs
1 cup sugar
3 tablespoons butter, melted
2 cups fresh or thawed frozen
   cranberries, coarsely
   chopped
1 cup walnuts, chopped
1 cup white chocolate chips

Preheat oven to 350°F. Spray 15×10×1-inch baking pan with cooking spray. In large bowl, beat flour, margarine, confectioners' sugar and salt at medium speed until mixture resembles coarse crumbs; press firmly and evenly into pan. Bake 20 minutes or until golden brown.

In large bowl, beat syrup, eggs, sugar and butter until well blended. Stir in cranberries and walnuts.

Spread mixture evenly over hot crust. Sprinkle white chocolate chips over top. Bake 25 to 30 minutes or until set. Cool completely on wire rack before cutting into bars.

Prep Time: 30 minutes • **Bake Time:** 45 to 50 minutes

Chocolate Cashew Coconut Bars

Makes 2½ dozen bars

1⅓ cups all-purpose flour
½ cup packed dark brown sugar
½ teaspoon baking powder
⅛ teaspoon salt
¾ cup (1½ sticks) unsalted butter, cubed, divided
1⅔ cups (10 ounces) finely chopped bittersweet chocolate

¾ cup whipping cream
½ cup granulated sugar
1 teaspoon vanilla
2 eggs
1½ cups flaked coconut
1½ cups chopped cashew nuts

1. Preheat oven to 350°F. Grease 13×9-inch baking pan.

2. Whisk flour, brown sugar, baking powder and salt in medium bowl; cut in ½ cup butter with pastry blender or two knives until mixture resembles coarse crumbs. Press into bottom of prepared pan. Bake 10 minutes or until set. Cool in pan on wire rack.

3. Place chocolate in medium bowl. Bring cream to a simmer in small heavy saucepan over medium-low heat. Pour over chocolate. Let stand 5 minutes; stir until smooth. Pour over crust. Refrigerate 15 minutes or until set.

4. Beat remaining ¼ cup butter in medium bowl with electric mixer at medium speed until light and fluffy. Add granulated sugar and vanilla; beat until blended. Add eggs, one at a time, beating well after each addition. Fold in coconut and cashews.

5. Spoon topping evenly over filling; gently spread over surface. Bake 25 minutes or until golden brown. Cool completely in pan on wire rack. Cut into bars.

Chocolate Crumb Bars

Makes 2½ dozen bars

1 cup (2 sticks) butter or margarine, softened
1¾ cups all-purpose flour
½ cup granulated sugar
¼ teaspoon salt
2 cups (12-ounce package) NESTLÉ® TOLL HOUSE® Semi-Sweet Chocolate Morsels, *divided*

1 can (14 ounces) NESTLÉ® CARNATION® Sweetened Condensed Milk
1 teaspoon vanilla extract
1 cup chopped walnuts (optional)

PREHEAT oven to 350°F. Grease 13×9-inch baking pan.

BEAT butter in large mixer bowl until creamy. Beat in flour, sugar and salt until crumbly. With floured fingers, press 2 cups crumb mixture onto bottom of prepared baking pan; reserve remaining mixture.

BAKE for 10 to 12 minutes or until edges are golden brown.

COMBINE 1 cup morsels and sweetened condensed milk in small, *heavy-duty* saucepan. Warm over low heat, stirring until smooth. Stir in vanilla extract. Spread over hot crust.

STIR nuts and *remaining* morsels into reserved crumb mixture; sprinkle over chocolate filling. Bake for 25 to 30 minutes or until center is set. Cool in pan on wire rack.

Lemon Iced Ambrosia Bars

Makes about 2½ dozen bars

1¾ cups all-purpose flour, divided
⅓ cup powdered sugar
¾ cup (1½ sticks) unsalted butter
2 cups packed light brown sugar

1 cup flaked coconut
1 cup finely chopped pecans
4 eggs, beaten
½ teaspoon baking powder
Lemon Icing (recipe follows)

1. Preheat oven to 350°F. Grease 13×9-inch baking pan.

2. Combine 1½ cups flour and powdered sugar in medium bowl; cut in butter with pastry blender or two knives until mixture resembles coarse crumbs. Press onto bottom of prepared pan; bake 15 minutes.

3. Meanwhile, combine remaining ¼ cup flour, brown sugar, coconut, pecans, eggs and baking powder in medium bowl; mix well. Spread evenly over baked crust; bake 20 minutes. Cool completely in pan on wire rack.

4. Prepare Lemon Icing; spread over filling. Cut into bars. Cover and refrigerate until ready to serve.

Lemon Icing: Stir together 2 cups powdered sugar, 3 tablespoons lemon juice and 2 tablespoons softened butter until smooth. Makes about ⅔ cup.

Brownies & Blondies

Double-Chocolate Pecan Brownies

Makes 9 brownies

¾ cup all-purpose flour

¾ cup unsweetened cocoa powder

½ cup CREAM OF WHEAT® Hot Cereal (Instant, 1-minute, 2½-minute or 10-minute cook time), uncooked

½ teaspoon baking powder

1¼ cups sugar

½ cup (1 stick) butter, softened

2 eggs

1 teaspoon vanilla extract

½ cup semisweet chocolate chips

½ cup pecans, chopped

1. Preheat oven to 350°F. Line 8-inch square baking pan with foil, extending foil over sides of pan; spray with nonstick cooking spray. Combine flour, cocoa, Cream of Wheat and baking powder in medium bowl; set aside.

2. Cream sugar and butter in large mixing bowl with electric mixer at medium speed. Add eggs and vanilla; mix until well combined.

3. Gradually add Cream of Wheat mixture; mix well. Spread batter evenly in pan, using spatula. Sprinkle chocolate chips and pecans evenly over top.

4. Bake 35 minutes. Let stand 5 minutes. Lift brownies from pan using aluminum foil. Cool completely before cutting.

Prep Time: 15 minutes • **Start-to-Finish Time:** 1 hour

Tip

For an even more decadent dessert, drizzle caramel sauce over the warm brownies and serve with mint chocolate chip ice cream.

MINI KISSES® Blondies

Makes about 3 dozen blondies

½ cup (1 stick) butter or margarine, softened
1⅓ cups packed light brown sugar
2 eggs
2 teaspoons vanilla extract
¼ teaspoon salt

2 cups all-purpose flour
1½ teaspoons baking powder
1¾ cups (10-ounce package) HERSHEY'S® MINI KISSES®BRAND Milk Chocolates
½ cup chopped nuts

1. Heat oven to 350°F. Lightly grease 13×9-inch baking pan.

2. Beat butter and brown sugar in large bowl until fluffy. Add eggs, vanilla and salt; beat until blended. Add flour and baking powder; beat just until blended. Stir in chocolate pieces. Spread batter in prepared pan. Sprinkle nuts over top.

3. Bake 28 to 30 minutes or until set and golden brown. Cool completely in pan on wire rack. Cut into bars.

Peppermint Brownies

Makes about 1½ dozen brownies

4 squares (1 ounce each)
    unsweetened baking
    chocolate

½ cup (1 stick) unsalted butter,
    softened

2 cups sugar

4 eggs

1 cup all-purpose flour

½ teaspoon peppermint
    extract

1 cup coarsely chopped
    walnuts (optional)

½ cup finely crushed
    peppermint candies*

About 18 peppermint candies will yield ½ cup finely crushed peppermints. To crush, place unwrapped candy in a heavy-duty resealable food storage bag. loosely seal the bag, leaving an opening for air to escape. Crush with a rolling pin, meat mallet or the bottom of a heavy skillet.

1. Preheat oven to 325°F. Grease 9-inch square baking pan.

2. Place chocolate and butter in medium microwavable bowl. Microwave on HIGH at 30-second intervals, stirring between each interval until melted and smooth.** Cool slightly.

3. Whisk sugar and eggs in large bowl until blended. Add chocolate mixture; mix well. Gradually add flour, stirring just until moistened. Fold in peppermint extract and walnuts, if desired. Spread batter in prepared pan.

4. Bake 35 minutes or until edges begin to pull away from sides of pan. Immediately sprinkle crushed candy over top. Cool completely in pan on wire rack. Cut into bars.

**Or combine chocolate and butter in top of double boiler over simmering water. Stir constantly until melted and smooth. Remove from heat immediately. Avoid getting any water in the chocolate or it will become brittle and hard.

Mocha Fudge Brownies

Makes about 1 dozen brownies

3 squares (1 ounce each) semisweet chocolate
¾ cup sugar
½ cup (1 stick) butter, softened
2 eggs
2 teaspoons instant espresso powder
1 teaspoon vanilla
½ cup all-purpose flour

½ cup chopped almonds, toasted*
1 cup (6 ounces) milk chocolate chips, divided

*To toast almonds, spread in single layer on baking sheet. Bake in preheated 350°F oven 8 to 10 minutes or until golden brown, stirring frequently.

1. Preheat oven to 350°F. Grease 8-inch square baking pan.

2. Melt semisweet chocolate in top of double boiler over simmering water. Remove from heat; cool slightly.

3. Beat sugar and butter in medium bowl with electric mixer at medium speed until light and fluffy. Add eggs, one at a time, beating well after each addition. Add chocolate, espresso powder and vanilla; beat until blended. Stir in flour, almonds and ½ cup chocolate chips. Spread batter in prepared pan.

4. Bake 25 minutes or until set. Sprinkle with remaining ½ cup chocolate chips. Let stand until melted; spread evenly over brownies. Cool completely in pan on wire rack. Cut into bars.

Tip

For easy removal, line the baking pan with foil and leave at least 2 inches hanging over each end. Use the foil to lift out the brownies, invert onto a cutting board and carefully remove the foil. Then cut into bars.

White Chocolate & Almond Blondies

Makes about 1½ dozen blondies

12 ounces white chocolate, broken into pieces
1 cup (2 sticks) unsalted butter
3 eggs

¾ cup all-purpose flour
1 teaspoon vanilla
½ cup slivered almonds

1. Preheat oven to 325°F. Grease and flour 9-inch square pan.

2. Melt white chocolate and butter in large heavy saucepan over low heat, stirring constantly. (White chocolate may separate.) Immediately remove from heat when chocolate is melted.

3. Add eggs; beat with electric mixer at medium speed until smooth. Beat in flour and vanilla. Spread batter in prepared pan. Sprinkle almonds over top.

4. Bake 30 minutes or until set. Cool completely in pan on wire rack. Cut into bars.

Fruit & Pecan Brownies

Makes about 1 dozen brownies

2 squares (1 ounce each) unsweetened chocolate
1 cup sugar
½ cup (1 stick) unsalted butter, softened
2 eggs
1 teaspoon vanilla

½ cup all-purpose flour
1 cup chopped dried mixed fruit
1 cup coarsely chopped pecans, divided
1 cup (6 ounces) semisweet chocolate chips, divided

1. Preheat oven to 350°F. Grease 8-inch square pan.

2. Melt unsweetened chocolate in top of double boiler over simmering water. Remove from heat; cool slightly.

3. Beat sugar and butter in large bowl with electric mixer at medium speed until light and fluffy. Add eggs, one at a time, beating well after each addition. Beat in chocolate and vanilla. Stir in flour, dried fruit, ½ cup pecans and ½ cup chocolate chips. Spread batter evenly in prepared pan. Sprinkle with remaining ½ cup pecans and ½ cup chocolate chips.

4. Bake 25 to 30 minutes or until center is set. Cover with foil while still warm. Cool completely in pan on wire rack. Cut into bars.

Tip

Pecans can be stored in an airtight container up to 3 months in the refrigerator and up to 6 months in the freezer.

Chunky Caramel Nut Brownies

Makes 2 dozen brownies

¾ cup (1½ sticks) butter
4 squares (1 ounce each)
  unsweetened chocolate
2 cups sugar
4 eggs
1 cup all-purpose flour
1 package (14 ounces)
  caramels

¼ cup whipping cream
2 cups pecan halves or
  coarsely chopped pecans,
  divided
1 package (12 ounces) milk
  chocolate chunks or chips,
  divided

1. Preheat oven to 350°F. Grease 13×9-inch baking pan.

2. Place butter and chocolate in large microwavable bowl. Microwave on HIGH 1½ to 2 minutes or until melted and smooth. Stir in sugar. Add eggs, one at a time, whisking well after each addition. Stir in flour. Spread half of batter in prepared pan. Bake 20 minutes.

3. Meanwhile, combine caramels and cream in medium microwavable bowl. Microwave on HIGH 1½ to 2 minutes or until caramels begin to melt; stir until melted and smooth. Stir in 1 cup pecans.

4. Spread caramel mixture over partially baked brownie layer. Sprinkle with half of chocolate chunks. Pour remaining brownie batter over top; sprinkle with remaining 1 cup pecan halves and chocolate chunks.

5. Bake 25 minutes or until set. Cool completely in pan on wire rack. Cut into bars.

White Chocolate Blondies

Makes about 2 dozen blondies

2 cups old-fashioned oats
1 cup all-purpose flour
1 cup white chocolate chips
1 cup packed brown sugar
1 teaspoon baking powder
1 teaspoon baking soda
1 teaspoon salt

¼ cup (½ stick) unsalted butter, softened
2 eggs
½ cup sweetened condensed milk
1 teaspoon vanilla

1. Preheat oven to 350°F. Grease 9-inch square baking pan.

2. Combine oats, flour, white chocolate chips, brown sugar, baking powder, baking soda and salt in large bowl. Beat butter, eggs, condensed milk and vanilla in medium bowl with electric mixer at medium speed until light and fluffy. Stir butter mixture into flour mixture until well blended. Press mixture into prepared pan.

3. Bake 25 to 30 minutes or until toothpick inserted into center comes out clean. Cool completely in pan on wire rack. Cut into squares.

Index

Acknowledgments

The publisher would like to thank the companies and organizations listed below for the use of their recipes and photographs in this publication.

ACH Food Companies, Inc.

Cream of Wheat® Cereal

Dole Food Company, Inc.

The Hershey Company

Nestlé USA

North Dakota Wheat Commission

The Quaker® Oatmeal Kitchens

Unilever

Metric Converstion Chart

VOLUME MEASUREMENTS (dry)

1/8 teaspoon = 0.5 mL
1/4 teaspoon = 1 mL
1/2 teaspoon = 2 mL
3/4 teaspoon = 4 mL
1 teaspoon = 5 mL
1 tablespoon = 15 mL
2 tablespoons = 30 mL
1/4 cup = 60 mL
1/3 cup = 75 mL
1/2 cup = 125 mL
2/3 cup = 150 mL
3/4 cup = 175 mL
1 cup = 250 mL
2 cups = 1 pint = 500 mL
3 cups = 750 mL
4 cups = 1 quart = 1 L

VOLUME MEASUREMENTS (fluid)

1 fluid ounce (2 tablespoons) = 30 mL
4 fluid ounces (1/2 cup) = 125 mL
8 fluid ounces (1 cup) = 250 mL
12 fluid ounces (1 1/2 cups) = 375 mL
16 fluid ounces (2 cups) = 500 mL

WEIGHTS (mass)

1/2 ounce = 15 g
1 ounce = 30 g
3 ounces = 90 g
4 ounces = 120 g
8 ounces = 225 g
10 ounces = 285 g
12 ounces = 360 g
16 ounces = 1 pound = 450 g

DIMENSIONS

1/16 inch = 2 mm
1/8 inch = 3 mm
1/4 inch = 6 mm
1/2 inch = 1.5 cm
3/4 inch = 2 cm
1 inch = 2.5 cm

OVEN TEMPERATURES

250°F = 120°C
275°F = 140°C
300°F = 150°C
325°F = 160°C
350°F = 180°C
375°F = 190°C
400°F = 200°C
425°F = 220°C
450°F = 230°C

BAKING PAN SIZES

Utensil	Size in Inches/Quarts	Metric Volume	Size in Centimeters
Baking or Cake Pan (square or rectangular)	8×8×2	2 L	20×20×5
	9×9×2	2.5 L	23×23×5
	12×8×2	3 L	30×20×5
	13×9×2	3.5 L	33×23×5
Loaf Pan	8×4×3	1.5 L	20×10×7
	9×5×3	2 L	23×13×7
Round Layer Cake Pan	8×1½	1.2 L	20×4
	9×1½	1.5 L	23×4
Pie Plate	8×1¼	750 mL	20×3
	9×1¼	1 L	23×3
Baking Dish or Casserole	1 quart	1 L	—
	1½ quart	1.5 L	—
	2 quart	2 L	—